SHECONOMY™

OCTOBER 2025

ADRIANA LUNA CARLOS
Editor-In-Chief, Designer
and Co-Founder

HANNA OLIVAS
Managing Editor &
Co-Founder

**ADVERTISING
OPPORTUNITIES**

Info@SheRisesStudios.com

SHECONOMY
OCTOBER 2025

**SHE RISES
STUDIOS**

CONTACT US

editorial@sherisesstudios.com

WWW.SHERISESSTUDIOS.COM

LETTER FROM THE EDITORS

Dear Reader,

Welcome to the October 2025 edition of Sheconomy™ Magazine, where we celebrate women shaping the future of our global economy. This month's theme, Building Wealth, Empowering Women: Driving Economic Change, highlights bold, innovative leaders redefining success on their own terms while uplifting others.

We are proud to feature Izabela Kvesic on our cover, a visionary entrepreneur, award-winning coach, and creator of the She Soars Collective. Her journey from corporate strategy to heart-led entrepreneurship embodies this edition's spirit, showing that true success is measured not just in numbers or titles, but in purpose, impact, and alignment. Izabela inspires women to activate their unique gifts, build authentic businesses, and lead with courage and confidence.

Inside, you'll meet remarkable individuals breaking barriers, innovating industries, and fostering inclusive economic growth. From strategies to scale businesses to stories of resilience and reinvention, each feature shows that entrepreneurship is about wealth, empowerment, and collective impact.

Sheconomy™ Magazine is more than a publication—it's a movement, a platform amplifying voices of vision, action, and inspiration. We hope this edition motivates you to dream boldly, act intentionally, and lead with heart. The next generation of changemakers is here, and their momentum is unstoppable.

Thank you for joining us in celebrating the leaders shaping a new economy.

Warm regards,

Adriana Luna Carlos & Hanna Olivas
Editors of Sheconomy™ Magazine

Become a
Managing Partner

Join a global Movement of Visionary Women
50+ Chapters. Transformative Community. Unlimited Growth.

WHAT'S INCLUDED

- 40% commission on memberships + event bonuses
- Leadership training, toolkits & ongoing support
- VIP access to retreats, masterminds & more

Join for just

www.shewinswomensnetwork.com

Application Fee (paid only after acceptance)

IZABELA KVESIC:
REDEFINING SUCCESS THROUGH PURPOSE, ALIGNMENT, AND HEART-LED LEADERSHIP

For nearly two decades, Izabela Kvesic thrived in corporate strategy. On paper, she was the definition of success climbing ranks, making an impact, and checking all the boxes of an accomplished career. But beneath the polished exterior, she felt an unsettling emptiness. She was living on autopilot, disconnected from her own heart. The pivotal moment came after another exhausting day of work followed by a grueling three-hour commute. As she tucked in her eight-year-old son, he asked her the question that pierced her soul: *"Mommy, why do you love your work more than me?"*

That moment was a wake-up call that Izabela could not ignore. *"It felt like a knife through my heart,"* she recalls. *"I knew I had to redefine what success meant for me and my family."* Stepping away from a comfortable but unfulfilling corporate career, she embarked on a new journey, one defined not by titles or paychecks, but by purpose, alignment, and impact. For Izabela, it was never just about leaving the corporate world behind. It was about moving toward a new definition of success, one that resonates with the soul and touches the lives of others.

At the heart of Izabela's mission is the belief that success means living in alignment with one's deepest values and gifts. She calls this *"activating your purpose."* To her, it isn't just about discovering what you're meant to do, it's about living it fully, out loud, every single day. *"Activating your purpose is when your values, your superpowers, and your actions all line up,"* she explains. *"It's not just knowing your purpose, it's embodying it through inspired action and a full heart."* In business, that means building services, products, and strategies that feel aligned and authentic, not forced. In life, it's reflected in the daily choices how one begins the morning, treats oneself, and loves others. For Izabela, purpose becomes real not through thoughts or plans, but through courageous, heart-led action.

Her passion for creating authentic spaces led to the founding of the She Soars Collective, a community designed to support women entrepreneurs. Unlike other groups that focus heavily on hustle, the She Soars Collective leads with heart. *"She Soars is about taking off the mask and being real about both the highs and the lows of entrepreneurship,"* she says. *"We grow together, not just in business strategy but in confidence and alignment."* One memorable session highlighted this difference. Instead of the usual introductions focused on titles and business achievements, Izabela asked participants to share a small mishap from their week. That moment of vulnerability broke down barriers instantly and allowed genuine connection to flourish. The Collective blends strategy and mindfulness, ensuring that women leave not only with clients and ideas, but also with confidence, focus, and a mindset shift that sustains them long after the meeting ends.

For Izabela, mindfulness isn't a side practice, it's the very thread that ties her leadership and coaching together. She teaches women to pause, reset, and reflect before rushing into action. From morning rituals to *"CEO Power Hours"* and energy audits, mindfulness serves as a compass, helping entrepreneurs move intentionally rather than reactively. Personally, she embodies this practice by deeply listening to her clients, creating space for clarity, and leading with presence. *"It's about being in the moment,"* she says, *"holding space so that others can find their own answers."*

Through her podcast, The Mindful Entrepreneur Talks, Izabela has created yet another avenue to inspire transformation. For her, the most rewarding moments come from the messages that say, *"I felt seen when I heard that episode."* One standout story involved a guest who had never appeared on video before, paralyzed by fear of being seen. But trusting Izabela's heart-led approach, she showed up authentically. Since then, that guest has blossomed embracing video, networking, and even speaking on stage. Watching her transformation confirmed for Izabela that storytelling has the power to ignite courage, action, and ripple effects far beyond a single conversation. *"That's the magic,"* she says with a smile.

As a recognized leader in brand building, Izabela distills her advice into one powerful truth: be unapologetically yourself. *"Your personal brand is simply your reputation made visible,"* she explains. *"It's the energy you carry into every interaction, every post, every stage. You don't need to be the loudest voice, you need to be the most authentic one."* When alignment is genuine, people can feel it. That trust, she says, is what attracts the right clients and opportunities.

Having spoken in 127 countries, Izabela has seen firsthand the universality of her message. Regardless of culture or geography, what resonates most is her reminder: *"You are more capable than you think you are."* She emphasizes that courage is built choice by choice, step by step. Across the globe, audiences light up when they realize their doubts do not define them, and their true power lies just beyond fear.

As a CEO, speaker, coach, and mother of three teenagers, Izabela knows the balancing act well. But she prefers the word *"harmony"* over *"balance."* *"Balance suggests a perfect equation, but harmony is a daily practice,"* she explains. She safeguards her time and energy through intentional routines, clear boundaries, and even a *"not-to-do"* list. Yet, she admits that some days are messy. *"The key is grace,"* she says. *"Grace for myself, asking for help, saying no when needed, and remembering that my kids are watching.*

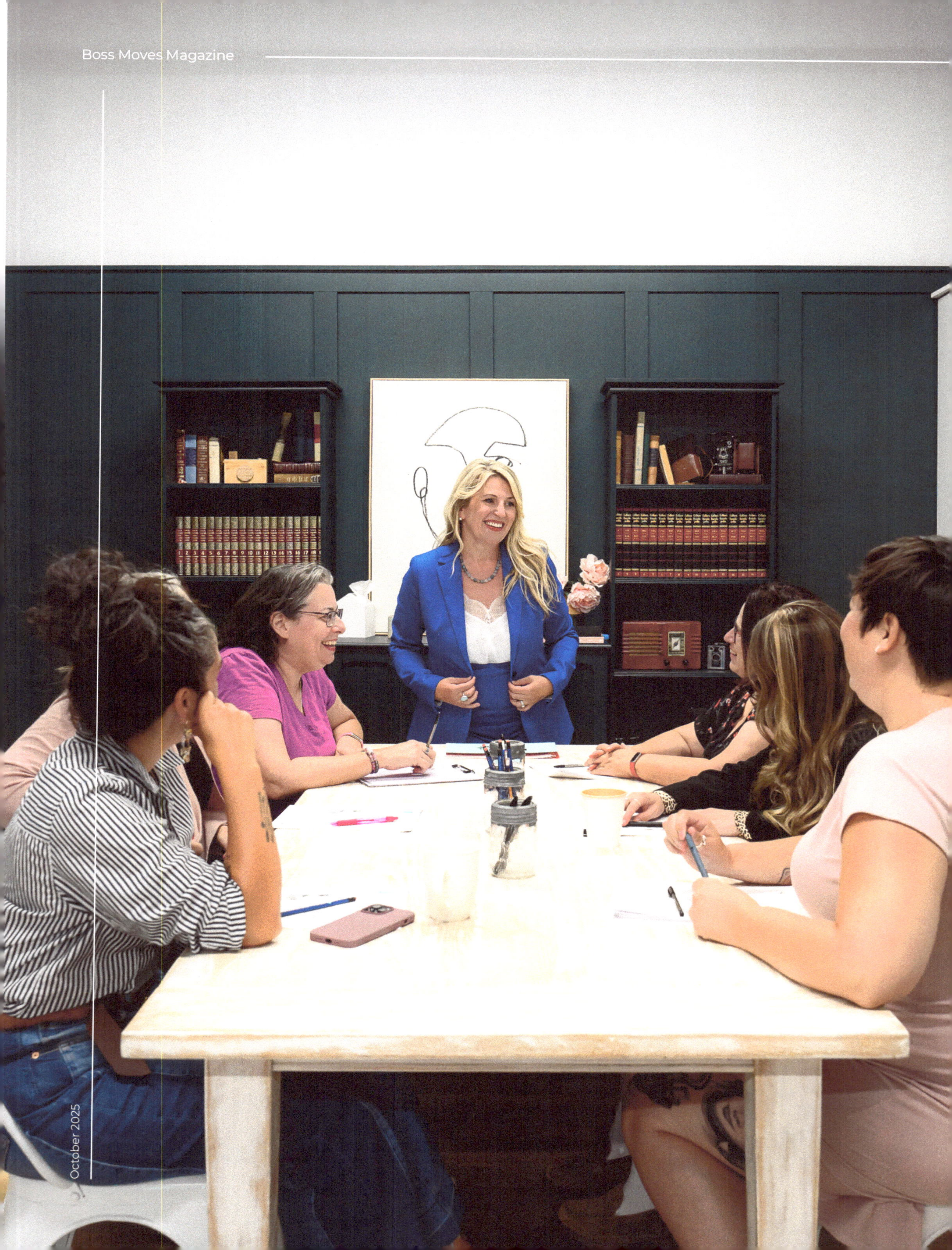

They're witnessing what it looks like to pursue dreams with courage and heart."

Izabela is currently working on her first book, She Soars (working title). Designed as a soulful guide for women entrepreneurs, it blends practical frameworks such as CEO Power Hours, Energy Audits, and the She Soars method with raw, personal stories of both the messy and magical moments of building an aligned business. Her hope is that the book becomes a trusted companion for women ready to embrace their power, grow boldly, and create success that feels authentic.

At the end of the day, Izabela's mission can be summed up in one simple yet profound phrase she often tells women: *"You got this."* But it isn't just about offering encouragement. She wants women to believe that everything they need strength, courage, creativity, and clarity already lies within them. Success isn't about perfection.

It's about trusting that their *"why"* is bigger than their fears and that the next aligned step forward is always within reach. That is where momentum begins. That is where the magic happens.

Through her coaching, the She Soars Collective, her podcast, and her upcoming book, Izabela Kvesic continues to redefine success for women across the globe one heart-led choice at a time.

Connect With Izabela

Instagram: @wearebluewater
www.bluewaterperformance.ca

BRUNCH & BOSS UP™

Brunch & Boss Up™ is not your average talk show—it's a bold, live YouTube experience filmed at high-energy brunch events across the U.S. Designed for the modern entrepreneur, each episode brings together a rotating cast of inspiring business owners, thought leaders, and creatives for real, unfiltered conversations in front of a live audience.

Expect candid stories, fun games, and breakthrough moments—served with mimosas, good food, and great company.

A LIVE BRUNCH SHOW ABOUT REAL ENTREPRENEURS, REAL STORIES, AND BOSS-LEVEL ENERGY

WHERE ELSE CAN YOU SIP MIMOSAS, SHARE STORIES, AND SPARK BREAKTHROUGHS OVER BRUNCH?

Brunch & Boss Up™ is a bold new live YouTube show filmed at high-energy brunch events across the U.S.—where entrepreneurs, creatives, and change-makers come together to eat, laugh, connect, and rise.

Hosted by Hanna Olivas and Adriana Luna Carlos, founders of She Rises Studios and FENIX TV, the show is a natural extension of their mission to empower women globally through storytelling, media, and community. Together, they create spaces where women feel seen, heard, and inspired to lead boldly.

Each episode is filmed in front of a live audience and features a rotating lineup of powerhouse guests who bring their stories, insights, and unfiltered truths to the table. It's where personality meets purpose, and where mimosas meet the mic.

From hilarious games and real conversations to unexpected breakthroughs, Brunch & Boss Up™ is equal parts fun, fierce, and uplifting.

Think Red Table Talk meets UpDating—with a shot of a mimosa and a whole lot of hustle.

Hosted by dynamic duo Hanna Olivas and Adriana Luna Carlos, the show brings their signature energy and heart to every city it touches. Each event is designed to celebrate connection, elevate voices, and create space for meaningful growth and collaboration.

Want to be part of the cast?

We're looking for 4–6 bold, dynamic entrepreneurs in each city to join the show.

As a featured cast member, you'll be:

- On stage, live with our hosts
- Part of the games, challenges, and conversations
- Featured on YouTube and across our social media
- Celebrated for your energy, personality, and story—not just your business

Brunch & Boss Up™ is coming to cities near you.

AMBITION

ANNE MAHLUM:

CRAFTING CHANGE THROUGH PURPOSE-DRIVEN ENTREPRENEURSHIP

Anne Mahlum is redefining the role of business as a force for good. As the founder of **The Little Market** and a series of community-focused ventures, she has built enterprises that blend entrepreneurship with social impact, empowering women artisans and supporting economic development globally. Mahlum's work perfectly embodies this October's *Sheconomy Magazine* theme, *"Building Wealth, Empowering Women: Driving Economic Change,"* demonstrating how vision, purpose, and leadership can create sustainable economic opportunities while advancing social change.

Mahlum's journey began with a desire to connect socially conscious consumers with fair-trade, handmade goods while creating economic opportunities for women around the world. In 2012, she co-founded **The Little Market**, an online marketplace that curates ethically made products from female artisans, prioritizing fair wages, transparency, and empowerment. The enterprise has grown into a platform that not only delivers beautiful products but also amplifies the stories and craftsmanship of the women behind them.

At the heart of Mahlum's mission is **women's economic empowerment**. By providing access to global markets and sustainable income, she helps women gain financial independence, build confidence, and cultivate entrepreneurial skills. The Little Market's model demonstrates that business can be both profitable and purposeful, proving that investing in women-led initiatives creates a ripple effect of opportunity that strengthens communities and drives lasting change.

Mahlum's ventures extend beyond commerce; they focus on fostering community, mentorship, and education. She leverages her platform to highlight the artistry, culture, and resilience of the women she works with, creating a narrative that emphasizes both economic and social value. By combining storytelling with commerce, Mahlum turns purchasing decisions into acts of empowerment, connecting consumers directly to meaningful impact.

Scaling purpose-driven businesses presents unique challenges, from navigating global supply chains to ensuring ethical standards are met consistently. Mahlum has addressed these challenges with strategic foresight, operational innovation, and a deep commitment to her mission. Her ability to balance profitability with social responsibility exemplifies the principles of modern, impact-oriented entrepreneurship, showing that businesses can thrive while serving a greater purpose.

The Little Market's success has inspired a broader ecosystem of community-focused ventures. Mahlum's leadership demonstrates that entrepreneurship can serve as a platform for systemic change, offering lessons on sustainability, ethical practices, and inclusive growth. Through workshops, mentorship programs, and speaking engagements, she actively encourages other entrepreneurs to embrace purpose-driven strategies that benefit both people and profit.

Beyond her companies, Mahlum advocates for **social entrepreneurship and women's leadership**. She emphasizes the importance of investing in female talent and creating opportunities that enable women to lead, innovate, and transform their communities. By combining advocacy with business practice, she reinforces the idea that economic empowerment and social impact are interconnected and mutually reinforcing.

Anne Mahlum's story illustrates the transformative potential of entrepreneurship guided by purpose. By creating platforms that uplift women artisans, generate sustainable income, and foster community engagement, she is shaping a new standard for business leadership. Her work proves that wealth, empowerment, and social responsibility can thrive together, demonstrating that women entrepreneurs are not just building companies—they are creating movements.

Through vision, creativity, and a relentless commitment to impact, Mahlum exemplifies how purpose-driven entrepreneurship can drive economic change while elevating communities and women worldwide. Her story is a powerful reminder that when business meets social good, the results are transformative, inspiring, and sustainable.

www.sherisesstudios.com

© COLLABORATIVE AGENCY GROUP

FROM IDEA TO EXECUTION

By **She Rises Studios Editorial Team**

Ambition without action is simply a dream. Turning ideas into execution is the cornerstone of effective leadership. Leaders who translate vision into tangible results combine planning, discipline, and adaptability to bring ideas to life.

Execution begins with clarity. Understanding the scope, goals, and desired outcomes of an idea provides direction and focus. Breaking a large concept into actionable steps ensures progress is measurable and sustainable.

Prioritization is critical. Not every idea is urgent or high-impact. Leaders who identify the tasks that most directly influence results allocate energy efficiently, avoiding wasted effort and maximizing returns.

Accountability drives execution. Setting deadlines, tracking progress, and reviewing outcomes hold both the leader and team responsible. Tools like project management platforms, scorecards, or regular check-ins enhance discipline and ensure milestones are met.

Adaptability is equally important. Execution rarely follows a linear path. Challenges, unforeseen obstacles, and new opportunities require flexible thinking and problem-solving. Leaders who adjust without losing sight of the ultimate goal maintain momentum and results.

Ultimately, the ability to turn ideas into action separates ambitious thinkers from successful doers. Leaders who combine clarity, prioritization, accountability, and adaptability transform ambition into measurable achievement.

> "Ideas become results when ambition meets disciplined execution."

RESILIENCE AS A BUSINESS STRATEGY

"Resilience turns obstacles into opportunities and ambition into lasting results."

By **She Rises Studios Editorial Team**

Setbacks are inevitable in leadership, but resilient leaders turn challenges into opportunities. Resilience is not just a personal trait—it's a strategic approach to sustaining progress, maintaining momentum, and achieving results.

Resilient leaders embrace challenges with perspective. Rather than seeing obstacles as failures, they view them as lessons that inform better decisions and sharpen focus. This mindset transforms adversity into advantage.

Emotional intelligence supports resilience. Leaders who manage stress, maintain composure, and respond thoughtfully to setbacks inspire confidence and stability in their teams. Calm, measured leadership encourages trust and collaborative problem-solving.

Resilience requires adaptability. Business environments evolve quickly, and leaders must pivot strategies, processes, and approaches without losing sight of their overarching goals. Flexibility ensures continuity and long-term success.

Persistence reinforces results. Leaders who sustain effort, overcome barriers, and continue learning demonstrate that setbacks are temporary and results are attainable. Their tenacity motivates teams and creates a culture of accountability and high performance.

Ultimately, resilience is a business strategy. Leaders who embrace challenges, adapt thoughtfully, and persevere strategically transform ambition into enduring results, proving that setbacks are merely stepping stones to success.

GRAB YOUR COPY NOW

Plan A Life You Love & Live It Out Loud Now: A Manifesto for Bold Women Ready to Stop Waiting and Start Living is a transformative guide for women ready to reclaim their power, purpose, and possibility. Blending memoir, guided journal, and legacy builder, it shares raw and inspiring stories of resilience alongside practical tools for living with clarity and courage. Each chapter offers honest breakthroughs, reflective prompts, and empowering strategies to help women embrace joy, align with their true values, and boldly define success on their own terms. With wisdom drawn from real experiences, this book reminds us that life is not about waiting—it's about choosing, creating, and living it out loud.

amazon.com   **SHE RISES STUDIOS**

GET YOUR COPY NOW

Celebrate the power of women through inspiring stories and insights.

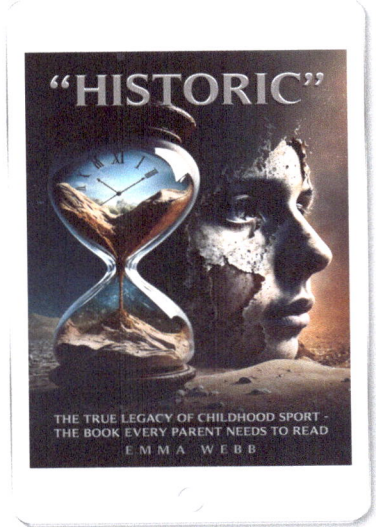

HISTORIC
EMMA WEBB

UPLIFT
ANA GOMES

MARTA: MARCIA. MARTKA.
MARTA SUCHOMSKA

TEACHING DURING THE PANDEMIC
DAWN SESSOM

T.R.I.B.E (TOUCH REQUIRES INTEGRITY AND
BOLDNESS EFFORTLESSLY)
DR. DOMINIQUE CARSON, LMP, MS

BORN TO FLOURISH
NANCY HILL

JESSICA MATTHEWS:

POWERING INNOVATION, EMPOWERING COMMUNITIES

Jessica Matthews is redefining the intersection of technology, sustainability, and economic empowerment. As the founder of **Uncharted Power**, she has built a company that not only develops innovative clean energy solutions but also creates economic opportunities for communities worldwide. Her work exemplifies this October's *Sheconomy Magazine* theme, *"Building Wealth, Empowering Women: Driving Economic Change,"* highlighting how women entrepreneurs are transforming industries while driving social and economic impact.

Matthews' journey began with a vision to address two critical global challenges simultaneously: access to clean energy and sustainable economic development. Through Uncharted Power, she designs scalable technologies that harness renewable energy, making electricity more accessible in underserved regions. These innovations have far-reaching implications—not only reducing environmental impact but also enabling communities to participate in the global economy more effectively.

At the core of Matthews' success is **innovative thinking paired with purposeful entrepreneurship**. Uncharted Power's solutions, such as kinetic energy-generating products and modular microgrids, demonstrate that clean technology can be both commercially viable and socially transformative. By bridging engineering excellence with a mission-driven approach, Matthews has positioned her company as a leader in the clean energy sector, proving that environmental responsibility and economic growth can coexist.

Matthews' leadership extends beyond technology. She prioritizes **creating opportunities for women and marginalized communities** in the fields of STEM, entrepreneurship, and energy development. Through mentorship programs, workforce training, and partnerships with local organizations, she ensures that her company's growth translates into broader social empowerment. Matthews' model shows that economic change is most impactful when it includes strategies to uplift others and foster inclusivity.

Scaling a clean energy business is not without challenges. Matthews navigated technical hurdles, investor skepticism, and the complexities of global market expansion while maintaining Uncharted Power's mission. Her resilience and strategic vision have been central to the company's success, illustrating that purposeful entrepreneurship requires both innovation and perseverance. Her ability to turn ideas into actionable, impactful solutions serves as a roadmap for women-led ventures seeking to combine profit with purpose.

Uncharted Power also demonstrates how mission-driven business models can attract investment while creating meaningful impact. Matthews has leveraged partnerships, grants, and investor networks to expand her company's reach, proving that women-led businesses can secure capital while staying true to social and environmental commitments. Her approach highlights the evolving landscape of entrepreneurship, where financial success and community benefit are increasingly intertwined.

Beyond her company, Matthews actively advocates for **sustainable innovation and women's economic participation**. She speaks at conferences, collaborates with global organizations, and mentors aspiring entrepreneurs, amplifying her influence across industries. Her commitment to both environmental and social outcomes reinforces the idea that leadership is measured not just by revenue,

© ICBA

but by the lasting positive change a company can generate.

Jessica Matthews' story is a testament to the power of visionary leadership. By developing clean energy solutions that empower communities and create economic opportunities, she exemplifies how women entrepreneurs are reshaping industries, driving innovation, and redefining the rules of business. Uncharted Power stands as a model for purposeful entrepreneurship, where financial growth and societal impact go hand in hand.

Through her work, Matthews demonstrates that women are not only capable of leading complex technological ventures but also of driving transformative economic and social change. She inspires a new generation of innovators to approach business with creativity, responsibility, and an unwavering commitment to making the world a better place —proving that wealth and empowerment can rise together.

www.sherisesstudios.com

MIKAILA ULMER:

SWEET SUCCESS WITH PURPOSE AND PASSION

© STYLEBLUEPRINT

At just a young age, Mikaila Ulmer transformed a simple idea into a thriving, socially conscious business. As the founder of **Me & the Bees Lemonade**, she has built more than a brand—she has created a platform for empowerment, environmental advocacy, and economic innovation. Her journey embodies this October's *Sheconomy Magazine* theme, *"Building Wealth, Empowering Women: Driving Economic Change,"* illustrating how entrepreneurial vision can merge profit with purpose to create lasting impact.

Ulmer's entrepreneurial story began when she was only four years old. Inspired by her grandmother's lemonade recipe and motivated by a passion for bees, she launched a lemonade stand with a mission: a portion of every sale would go toward **bee preservation**.

Her early commitment to social impact laid the foundation for a business that has since grown into a nationally recognized brand, sold in grocery stores across the United States and supported by major investors and mentors, including the renowned *Shark Tank* investors who helped bring her vision to scale.

What sets Mikaila apart is her ability to combine **entrepreneurial savvy with purpose-driven leadership**. Me & the Bees Lemonade is more than a beverage company; it is a testament to how business can be a force for good. By allocating resources to environmental conservation, Ulmer ensures that her company's growth contributes to a greater mission. This focus on social responsibility resonates with consumers and investors alike, proving that conscious business models are not only ethically sound but economically viable.

Scaling her business at such a young age required resilience, creativity, and a willingness to learn from challenges. Ulmer faced obstacles typical of any startup—logistical hurdles, marketing complexities, and production scaling —but she approached each challenge with strategic thinking and determination. Her success demonstrates that entrepreneurship is as much about mindset as it is about ideas: the courage to act, the discipline to persist, and the vision to see opportunities where others might see risk.

Ulmer also embodies the essence of **women-driven economic empowerment**. By leading a nationally recognized company as a young female entrepreneur of color, she inspires a new generation of girls and women to see themselves as capable leaders and innovators. Her story shows that age and background do not limit potential and that women-led businesses can thrive while advancing social good. Through mentorship opportunities, speaking engagements, and media presence, Ulmer actively encourages other young entrepreneurs to pursue their ideas with confidence and purpose.

Beyond her business achievements, Mikaila leverages her platform to raise awareness about **critical environmental issues**. She educates consumers about the importance of bees to ecosystems and food supply chains, turning a commercial product into a tool for advocacy and education. This integration of mission and entrepreneurship highlights her holistic approach to leadership: success is measured not only by revenue but by the positive impact generated for people and the planet.

Mikaila Ulmer's journey proves that building wealth and driving social change are not mutually exclusive. Me & the Bees Lemonade stands as a model of **entrepreneurial innovation, purpose-driven strategy, and community impact**. By blending profitability with environmental advocacy, she has created a business that empowers women, supports sustainable practices, and inspires countless young entrepreneurs to turn their ideas into meaningful ventures.

Through her unwavering commitment to innovation, social responsibility, and empowerment, Mikaila Ulmer exemplifies what it means to lead with purpose. Her story reminds us that women driving economic change are not just shaping industries—they are rewriting the rules of business, proving that entrepreneurship can be a powerful catalyst for impact, opportunity, and collective growth.

© AUDIBLE

RESHMA SAUJANI:

CODING A FUTURE OF EMPOWERMENT AND OPPORTUNITY

Reshma Saujani is redefining what it means to empower the next generation of women in the digital economy. As the founder of **Girls Who Code**, she has built a movement that equips young women with critical technology skills, bridging the gender gap in tech and creating pathways for economic empowerment. Her work exemplifies this October's *Sheconomy Magazine* theme, *"Building Wealth, Empowering Women: Driving Economic Change,"* highlighting how visionary leaders can foster both social and economic transformation.

Saujani's journey began with a recognition of the persistent gender disparities in technology and entrepreneurship. She noticed that while the tech industry was booming, women and girls were severely underrepresented in programming and computer science roles. Determined to address this imbalance, she founded Girls Who Code in 2012, providing educational programs, mentorship, and resources designed specifically to inspire young women to enter and thrive in the tech world.

At the heart of Saujani's mission is **economic empowerment through skill-building**. By equipping girls with coding abilities, critical thinking skills, and confidence, Girls Who Code opens doors to high-demand careers in technology—sectors that have traditionally been male-dominated and economically lucrative. Through this work, Saujani demonstrates that closing the gender gap in tech is not only a matter of equality but also a driver of economic growth and innovation.

The organization's programs, ranging from after-school clubs to intensive summer immersion courses, emphasize practical learning and real-world application. Girls participate in coding projects, build apps, and collaborate on solutions to societal challenges, gaining hands-on experience that prepares them for future careers. Saujani's approach ensures that participants are not just learning technical skills—they are developing leadership qualities, resilience, and the entrepreneurial mindset essential for long-term success.

Saujani's leadership extends beyond program development. She actively advocates for policy changes, industry partnerships, and public awareness campaigns to support gender equity in technology. Her voice amplifies the economic and societal benefits of investing in women's tech education, showing that when young women are empowered to innovate, entire industries and communities benefit. By combining grassroots action with systemic advocacy, she maximizes the impact of her mission.

Girls Who Code has reached tens of thousands of students across the United States and beyond, proving that structured education, mentorship, and encouragement can dismantle barriers and cultivate opportunity. By focusing on inclusivity and accessibility, Saujani ensures that girls from diverse backgrounds gain equitable access to high-quality tech education. This commitment underscores her belief that economic empowerment must be available to all, regardless of socioeconomic status, ethnicity, or geography.

Saujani's work highlights the broader ripple effects of empowering women in technology. Graduates of Girls Who Code are entering the workforce with competitive skills, contributing to innovation, and driving economic activity. They are also serving as role models and mentors, inspiring future generations to pursue tech careers, creating a sustainable cycle of empowerment, leadership, and economic participation.

Reshma Saujani's story exemplifies how vision, leadership, and action can transform not only individual lives but entire industries. By providing young women with the tools, knowledge, and confidence to succeed in tech, she is cultivating economic impact, fostering innovation, and reshaping the future of work. Girls Who Code stands as a model of how women-driven initiatives can drive both empowerment and economic growth.

Through her tireless efforts, Saujani demonstrates that empowering women with skills, opportunities, and confidence is a powerful strategy for driving lasting economic change. She proves that when women rise in technology, they uplift communities, industries, and the broader economy—showing that wealth, impact, and empowerment can grow hand in hand.

www.sherisesstudios.com

© AUDIBLE

SHOP NOW

GRAB YOUR COPY NOW

Becoming An Unstoppable Woman: Rise of the Phoenix is an empowering anthology for women who have faced adversity and chosen to rise stronger than ever. As the third installment in the bestselling series, it features raw, unfiltered stories of resilience, reinvention, and the unbreakable spirit of women who refused to be defined by their struggles. From battles with health and relationships to challenges in careers and identity, each chapter offers powerful lessons of courage and transformation. Through honesty and hope, these women light the path for others navigating life's darkest moments. With wisdom drawn from real experiences, this book reminds us that even from the ashes, we can rise, reclaim our power, and soar as unstoppable women.

amazon.com   **SHE RISES** STUDIOS

GET YOUR COPY NOW

Celebrate the power of women through inspiring stories and insights.

RENAISSANCE: REDEFINING SUCCESS
FOR MODERN MAVERICKS
MELISSA AARSKAUG & MICHELE KLINE

THE UNLEARNED LIFE: A SELF-GUIDED
SYSTEM FOR WOMEN READY TO HEAL, LEVEL
UP, AND ACTIVATE THEIR SOUL'S CALLING
KATHY BALDWIN

IN PURSUIT OF PLEASURE: TALES OF SEXUAL
AWAKENING, FINDING CONFIDENCE, AND
LIVING UNAPOLOGETICALLY
RACHEL STREVENS

NAKED! WOMANIZER
ANNAMARIA SOLANA
(ANNAMARIA BEREK)

LIVING FROM SOUL
ELEANOR HASPEL-PORTNER

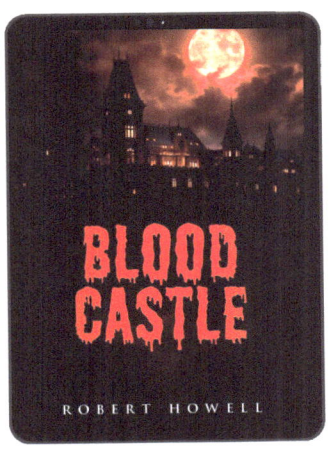

BLOOD CASTLE
ROBERT HOWELL

EXPLOSIVE CONNECTIONS:
BUILDING BUSINESS THROUGH
STRATEGIC RELATIONSHIPS
JANELLE KENNEDY

WHITNEY WOLFE HERD:
PIONEERING CONNECTIONS, EMPOWERING WOMEN

© IMDB

Whitney Wolfe Herd has transformed the way the world connects, networks, and engages socially and professionally. As the founder and CEO of **Bumble**, she has reimagined the digital landscape by creating a platform that prioritizes women's agency, empowerment, and leadership. Herd's innovative approach embodies this October's *Sheconomy Magazine* theme, *"Building Wealth, Empowering Women: Driving Economic Change,"* highlighting how women-led companies can revolutionize industries while fostering social impact and economic growth.

Herd's journey began with a vision to challenge the norms of online dating. Recognizing that traditional platforms often perpetuated imbalances in communication and safety, she launched Bumble in 2014 with a simple yet transformative idea: **empower women to make the first move**. This approach not only disrupted the dating industry but also set a new standard for digital interaction, creating a safer and more equitable environment for users worldwide.

Bumble quickly evolved beyond dating. Herd expanded the platform to include **Bumble BFF** for friendships and **Bumble Bizz** for professional networking, cementing her company's position as a multi-dimensional social network. By integrating business, social, and personal connections into one platform, Herd has built a thriving ecosystem that encourages women to engage, lead, and create opportunities across multiple facets of life. Her vision demonstrates that innovation, when guided by purpose, can drive both social empowerment and economic influence.

What sets Herd apart is her commitment to **women-focused leadership and corporate responsibility**. Bumble is not only designed to empower users but also embodies Herd's principles internally. She has cultivated a workplace culture that prioritizes inclusivity, equality, and growth, ensuring that women thrive at all levels of the organization. This holistic approach to leadership reinforces the company's mission and serves as a model for women-led enterprises worldwide.

Scaling Bumble to a publicly traded company at such a young age required strategic acumen, resilience, and courage. Herd navigated the complexities of venture capital, technology innovation, and global market expansion while maintaining the company's core mission. Her success demonstrates that women-led businesses can compete at the highest levels, influence industry standards, and drive measurable economic change while remaining true to their values.

Beyond business, Herd uses her platform to champion broader **social initiatives**. From advocating for gender equality and women's rights to supporting community programs that promote empowerment and mentorship, she amplifies the impact of her work beyond the digital space. Her leadership proves that corporate success and social responsibility are not mutually exclusive—they are intertwined components of sustainable, purpose-driven entrepreneurship.

Whitney Wolfe Herd's story illustrates the power of vision, innovation, and intentional leadership. By redefining how women interact socially and professionally, she has created a company that elevates both individual users and the broader economic landscape. Bumble stands as a testament to the potential of women-led ventures to disrupt industries, create opportunities,

and set new standards for inclusion and empowerment.

Through her entrepreneurial journey, Herd shows that building wealth and driving social impact can go hand in hand. She proves that women entrepreneurs are not only capable of achieving financial success but also of reshaping industries, inspiring communities, and empowering future generations to lead boldly and purposefully. Whitney Wolfe Herd exemplifies the next generation of business leaders who are changing the rules of the game, one connection at a time.

www.sherisesstudios.com

© TIM FERRISS

UNIVERSITY OF LEEDS

ENROLL FREE TODAY TO SCALE YOUR BUSINESS

She Rises Studios and Goldman Sachs 10,000 Women join forces to provide education, resources, and a supportive global community for women-led SMEs, empowering them to grow, innovate, and thrive in today's competitive landscape.

she wins

WOMEN'S NETWORK

Elevate your business with the power of community.

Get access to the tools, connections, and support you need to grow—with a circle of women who truly get it.

WHAT'S INCLUDED

- Strategic networking & mentorship
- Expert-led masterclasses & exclusive resources
- Member spotlights, VIP perks & more

Join for just

$87/MONTH

no contracts, cancel anytime.

www.shewinswomensnetwork.com

THE ART OF NEGOTIATION

By **She Rises Studios Editorial Team**

> "Negotiation is the bridge between ambition and measurable success."

Negotiation is a critical skill for ambitious leaders. The ability to advocate, influence, and reach mutually beneficial agreements turns opportunity into measurable results, creating advantage in business and life.

Preparation is key. Effective negotiators understand their goals, value proposition, and potential outcomes before entering discussions. Researching counterparts, market conditions, and alternatives builds confidence and leverage.

Active listening enhances negotiation outcomes. Understanding the other party's needs and motivations uncovers opportunities for win-win solutions. Leaders who listen attentively demonstrate respect, credibility, and strategic insight.

Confidence and assertiveness matter. Clearly articulating value, priorities, and boundaries communicates professionalism and influence. Ambitious leaders balance firmness with flexibility, ensuring agreements align with objectives.

Follow-through ensures results. Negotiation does not end with an agreement—it requires implementation, accountability, and relationship management. Leaders who maintain integrity and consistency reinforce trust and long-term impact.

Ultimately, mastering negotiation transforms ambition into tangible outcomes. Leaders who prepare, listen, communicate confidently, and execute agreements create results that reflect vision, strategy, and influence.

LEVERAGING NETWORKS FOR OPPORTUNITY

By **She Rises Studios Editorial Team**

> ## "Strong networks turn ambition into opportunity and potential into results."

Ambition grows exponentially when paired with strategic relationships. Leaders who cultivate, nurture, and leverage networks convert opportunities into measurable outcomes, gaining access to resources, partnerships, and insights.

Networking begins with intentionality. Identifying connections aligned with goals and values ensures relationships are meaningful and mutually beneficial. Leaders who invest in purposeful connections create platforms for collaboration and growth.

Value exchange strengthens networks. Leaders offer support, insight, and expertise while seeking guidance, introductions, or collaboration. This reciprocal approach builds trust and strengthens long-term relationships.

Mentorship and peer networks amplify influence. Learning from experienced professionals, sharing knowledge, and seeking diverse perspectives accelerates decision-making and strategic impact. Leaders gain guidance while positioning themselves as influential contributors.

Effective networking requires consistency. Regular engagement, follow-up, and visibility maintain relationships and unlock new opportunities. Leaders who communicate authentically and deliver value solidify their credibility and expand reach.

Ultimately, networks convert ambition into tangible results. Leaders who cultivate meaningful relationships access insights, opportunities, and partnerships that drive measurable success and long-term growth.

LEVELING THE PLAYING FIELD:

HOW MULIER FORTIS IS DRIVING INVESTMENT INTO WOMEN'S SPORTS

By **Raquel Braun and Lagen Nash**

To start things off... we are Raquel Braun and Lagen Nash, the Co-Founders of Mulier Fortis, which means "Strong Woman" in Latin. We created Mulier Fortis to address a critical gap: the need for dedicated executive leadership and expertise in sports, entertainment, and technology. Between us, we brought forty years of experience navigating some of the world's biggest sports and media stages - Raquel as a lawyer and industry veteran shaping groundbreaking partnerships at EA Sports, Women's Sports Network, and FOX Sports, and Lagen as a dynamic business leader driving growth at Misfits Gaming, Silver Tribe Media, and FOX. Together, we envisioned a hybrid firm offering high-level strategy and operational solutions which led us to Mulier Fortis.

Mulier Fortis drives economic growth by providing fractional C-suite expertise and securing lucrative media rights, sponsorships, and partnerships for women's sports leagues and emerging organizations, while also attracting private equity investment into these underserved markets. We champion representation through our women-led, women-first approach, elevating female athletes' market value and advocating for inclusive leadership and equitable opportunities within the industry. This strategic focus, combined with our cross-industry reach in sports, media, and technology, allows us to significantly influence how women's sports are commercialized, consumed, and perceived, ultimately reshaping the industry's landscape.

Growth and representation in sports, specifically in women's sports is important right now because the industry is at a tipping point. Global demand for women's sports content is surging, with record-breaking attendance, rising media rights values, and sponsorship ROI that often outpaces men's sports in engagement per dollar. Yet, structural inequities, lower investment, fewer leadership opportunities, and limited visibility still hold the space back. By prioritizing growth and representation, organizations like Mulier Fortis help capture this momentum, ensuring women athletes and leagues aren't just included but valued as core drivers of the sports economy. This isn't only about fairness; it's a business imperative as fans, brands, and investors increasingly demand diversity, equity, and authentic representation in the properties they support.

The future of women's sports holds tremendous opportunity: a landscape where female athletes, leagues, and executives have equal access to resources, visibility, and investment as their male counterparts. The hope is that women's sports will no longer be seen as a *"niche,"* but as a mainstay in the global sports economy, driving growth, fan engagement, and cultural influence. In this future, women's sports will command competitive media rights deals, establish sustainable leagues with robust sponsorship portfolios, and inspire the next generation of athletes and leaders. Mulier Fortis is poised to play a catalytic role in that evolution, bridging institutional gaps, elevating representation in leadership, and fostering authentic partnerships that not only grow women's sports commercially but also redefine their place in the broader cultural and business landscape.

Moving forward, our primary goal is to continue partnering with exceptional clients, guiding them through strategic scaling and growth initiatives. The most rewarding aspect of our work is witnessing these organizations achieve significant milestones and realize their full potential.

Connect With Us

www.wearemulierfortis.com
www.instagram.com/wearemulierfortis

FENIX TV
YOUR PLATFORM, YOUR VOICE, YOUR POWER!

STEP INTO THE SPOTLIGHT AS A HOST ON FENIX TV!

Are you ready to amplify your message, inspire others, and be part of a groundbreaking network dedicated to empowering women worldwide? FENIX TV is your platform to shine as a host, share your expertise, and connect with a global audience.

WHY HOST ON FENIX TV?

- Reach a worldwide audience passionate about empowerment
- Showcase your voice, brand, and expertise
- Join a community of inspiring leaders and changemakers
- Be part of a network that uplifts and celebrates women

Whether you dream of leading a talk show, sharing powerful stories, or educating and inspiring others—FENIX TV is where your voice matters!

SECURE YOUR SPOT TODAY!

 Contact us now at
info@fenixtv.app

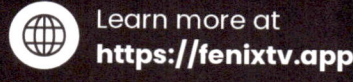 Learn more at
https://fenixtv.app

A NEW ERA IN WHAT YOU WEAR:

BECAUSE THE ATHLETE IN ALL OF US DESERVES BETTER - IT'S TIME YOUR CLOTHES WORK FOR YOU.

By **Megan Brown**

I've been an athlete all my life. Even competing at the highest level while in college. After graduating, I approached everything in my life as an athlete. Instead of running on the turf, I was running down the *"financial"* streets of business. Then I was running my kids to school, running to keep up with my career, running to hold my family together. My entire life has been about motion, about pushing forward, about finding a way to keep going no matter the challenge.

But when I lost my thyroid and had my third child later in life, even I felt like I couldn't keep up.

My body, schedule, and confidence all felt foreign. Suddenly, the simple act of carving out time for myself felt impossible.

Everywhere I turned, I was told I had to choose: get back into shape or be fully present as a wife and mother. That *"choice"* didn't sit right with me. Why couldn't I have both?

That's when I realized I didn't need more hours in the day. I needed a smarter way to use the ones I already had. I wasn't going to wait for someone else to create it.

I was going to do it myself.

That was the spark for KILOGEAR. I created the first real clothing line designed with built-in, removable MICRO weights that transform everyday movement into strength training. Walking the dog, cooking dinner, sitting at my desk, traveling, coaching on the field… all of it could now count. My life didn't need to stop so I could work out. My life was the workout.

Building Something No One Believed In

Starting KILOGEAR was like stepping back into the competitive arena, except this time the playing field was a male-dominated sports and fitness industry. I was a woman with no apparel experience with an idea no one had seen before. Manufacturers told me it couldn't be done. Potential partners didn't understand it. Investors wanted proof before they'd commit.

There were nights I wondered if the skeptics were right. But I leaned in: you don't quit when it's hard. You push back.

I obsessed over fabrics, comfort, and design, testing prototypes with athletes, moms, dads, professionals, doctors, nurses, teachers, anyone who wanted to get more out of their time and life. Every small win became fuel: a teenage athlete improving her sprint speed, a busy mom losing weight without ever stepping foot in a gym, a coach calling it a *"game-changer."*

Expanding the Impact

Fast forward to today, where you can find KILOGEAR at Free People Movement and Equinox Gyms. KILOGEAR is used by professional athletes, elite academies, aging athletes, youth teams, and everyday people around the world. But KILOGEAR isn't just about athletes. It's about everyday people turning life into fitness. Busy parents wear it while working from home or doing chores. Corporate employees wear it during conferences and *"fit breaks"* at hotels. And older adults use it to preserve muscle, bone density, and independence as they age.

We even work with physicians, including pediatricians and sports medicine specialists, who recommend KILOGEAR as a proactive way to keep kids and teens healthy. From the very beginning, I knew efficacy had to be the cornerstone of our brand. My very first hire was a doctor because I wanted to ensure that every product we created was both safe and proven to work. No other company in this space has the testing or efficacy validation that KILOGEAR has.

Why This Matters

Weight loss and fitness are often framed around restriction (less food, less time, less joy). But KILOGEAR is about addition. Adding strength. Adding confidence. Adding health. Adding years of independence for older adults.

We're living in a time where people sit more, move less, and feel busier than ever. For many, the idea of carving out an hour at the gym feels unrealistic. But what if you didn't need to? What if you could just put on clothes that made every step, every task, every movement count? That's what KILOGEAR does.

Our motto is simple: don't change your life, just change your clothes.

Women Leading in Sports and Business

Women have always been known for reinventing the way things are done, often because we're the ones living the inefficiencies every day. The dishwasher, the ironing board, disposable diapers, even correction fluid were all created by women who saw a better way to make life work. KILOGEAR is part of that same tradition. I was living the challenge of trying to stay strong while balancing career and family, and I built a smarter solution: clothing that works for you while you live your life. For me, shaping the business of sports means building something that didn't exist, overcoming countless roadblocks, and proving that women can not only compete but dominate in spaces that weren't designed for us.

We make gear for men, women, boys and girls. However, so much of training gear has been designed for male athletes, from the design and fit, to the performance features. Female athletes have historiclaly had far fewer options. At KILOGEAR, we are changing that by designing products made specifically for the female body and the way women move, train, and live.

I didn't just want a seat at the table. I built my own table, and now I'm pulling up chairs for others.

KILOGEAR is proof that innovation in sports can come from outside the traditional power structures. It can come from women. It can come from mothers who are tired of impossible choices. And it can come from athletes who understand that the real sport is the sport of life. Just because you stop competing for medals or wins doesn't mean you stop competing. You can continue to contribute, to build, to lead, and to make an impact long after your playing days are over.

Megan Brown is the Founder of KILOGEAR, the first MICRO weighted apparel company. She partners with athletes, coaches, and medical professionals worldwide to redefine training and wellness by turning everyday movement into performance. Megan is passionate about helping women, families, and athletes of all ages build strength, resilience, and confidence.

Connect With Megan

www.kilogear.com
Instagram: @KILOGEAR @KILOGEARPRO
www.linkedin.com/in/mrsmeganbrown

THE SHE RISES STUDIOS
PODCAST

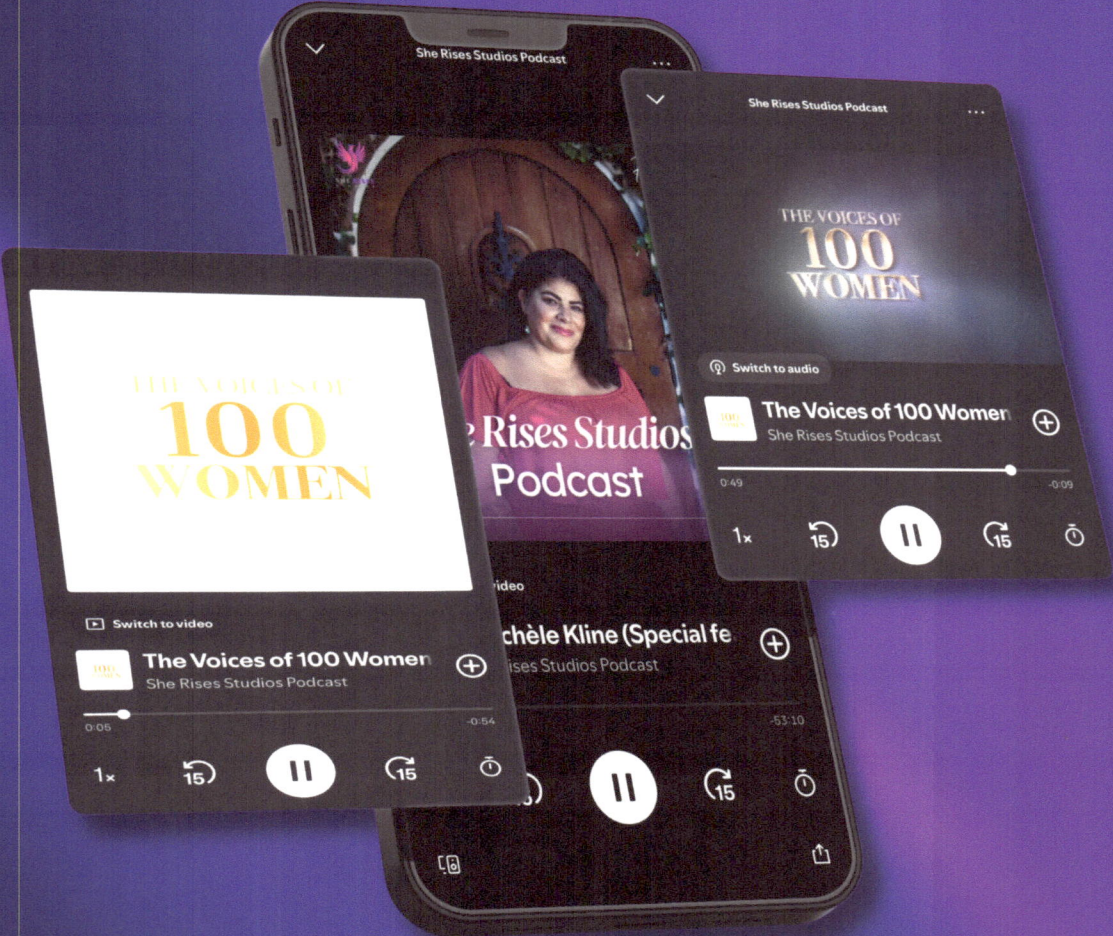

Each episode of the She Rises Studios Podcast delivers real stories, expert insights, and actionable strategies to help you step into your power and create the life you desire. This isn't just a podcast—it's your roadmap to confidence, success, and purpose.

Through powerful interviews with trailblazing entrepreneurs, thought leaders, and inspiring women, we dive deep into conversations that spark growth, fuel ambition, and ignite your potential. If you're ready to rise higher and live boldly, you're in the right place.

SUBSCRIBE NOW AND START YOUR JOURNEY TO EMPOWERMENT!

JOIN THE SHE RISES STUDIOS COMMUNITY

SCAN TO JOIN

Daily motivation, expert insights, and sisterhood support come together in one empowering space. Connect, empower, and thrive—whether you're an entrepreneur, professional, or simply seeking inspiration, this is your place to grow!

You don't have to do it alone—let's rise together!

MASTERING TIME FOR MAXIMUM IMPACT

By **She Rises Studios Editorial Team**

> "Time mastered is ambition realized—focus fuels measurable results."

Time is the most valuable resource for ambitious leaders. Mastering it is essential for turning goals into results. Effective time management ensures productivity, focus, and the ability to execute on high-priority objectives.

Start with prioritization. Identify tasks that directly impact results and focus energy there. Techniques such as the Eisenhower Matrix help distinguish between urgent and important activities, allowing leaders to allocate time strategically.

Block scheduling is another powerful tool. Designating dedicated time for deep work, creative projects, and decision-making minimizes distractions and enhances output. Leaders who protect these blocks create consistent progress toward objectives.

Delegation amplifies impact. Recognizing which tasks can be entrusted to others frees up energy for high-value responsibilities. Empowering teams not only improves efficiency but also develops future leaders.

Mindful breaks support sustained productivity. Short pauses throughout the day prevent burnout, improve focus, and foster innovation. Ambitious leaders recognize that balance and recovery are critical for consistent performance.

Ultimately, mastering time transforms ambition into results. Leaders who prioritize, schedule strategically, delegate wisely, and practice self-care achieve maximum impact, turning each hour into progress.

> **"Smart decisions turn ambition into measurable growth and lasting impact."**

STRATEGIC DECISION-MAKING FOR GROWTH

By **She Rises Studios Editorial Team**

Ambition without strategic decision-making risks wasted energy and missed opportunities. Leaders who make informed, intentional choices convert potential into measurable outcomes, accelerating growth and impact.

Strategic decisions begin with clarity of purpose. Understanding organizational or personal objectives ensures choices align with long-term vision. Leaders avoid reactionary thinking, instead approaching challenges with foresight and analysis.

Gathering data and insights strengthens decision-making. Market trends, competitor analysis, and performance metrics provide a foundation for informed choices. Leaders who balance intuition with evidence optimize outcomes while minimizing risk.

Scenario planning enhances readiness. Considering multiple outcomes and potential obstacles prepares leaders to pivot efficiently. Strategic thinkers anticipate challenges, ensuring adaptability while maintaining momentum toward results

Collaboration enriches decisions. Consulting with team members, mentors, or stakeholders provides diverse perspectives, uncovering blind spots and innovative solutions. Leadership that leverages collective wisdom increases both buy-in and effectiveness.

Ultimately, strategic decision-making transforms ambition into growth. Leaders who combine purpose, insight, planning, and collaboration create measurable outcomes, proving that results come from thoughtful action, not mere desire.

SHEWINS
GLOBAL SUMMIT

Step into a transformative 2-day experience where 300+ women entrepreneurs, leaders, and innovators unite for empowerment, collaboration, and celebration.

Expect an unforgettable experience with 20+ dynamic speakers and panels featuring thought leaders, experts, and change-makers. Enjoy celebrity fireside chats, a red carpet experience with media coverage and networking, and interactive main stage sessions designed to equip you with powerful strategies for unstoppable growth while connecting with powerhouse women worldwide.

TICKETS AND SPEAKER APPLICATIONS NOW OPEN
VISIT SHERISESSTUDIOS.COM TO SECURE YOUR SPOT

LAS VEGAS, NEVADA I NOVEMBER 6–7, 2025

𝒰NLEASH YOUR STORY

BECOME A PUBLISHED AUTHOR!

Have you ever dreamed of sharing your wisdom, experience, or passion with the world? **Now is your time!**

Publishing a book isn't just about writing—it's about **establishing your authority, inspiring others, and creating a lasting legac**y. Plus, with the **$138.5 billion book industry** booming, there's never been a better moment to step into the spotlight.

At **SRS Publishing**, we don't just publish books—we **elevate voices, empower authors, and create change-makers**. Our mission is to help women break barriers, amplify their stories, and thrive in the publishing world. Whether you're an entrepreneur, thought leader, or storyteller at heart, **we're here to guide you every step of the way.**

JOIN THE FASTEST-GROWING PUBLISHING HOUSE FOR WOMEN IN THE USA.

READY TO TURN YOUR DREAM INTO REALITY?

 www.SheRisesStudios.com | contact@sherisesstudios.com

100
WOMEN OF IMPACT™
THE DOCUSERIES THAT AMPLIFIES WOMEN'S VOICES

We just wrapped our first taping of 100 Women of Impact™ in San Diego, and the momentum has only just begun. This powerful docuseries is shining a spotlight on extraordinary women who are shaping the future through leadership, resilience, and influence.

Be part of the movement by sharing your story in an exclusive filmed interview for the docuseries. Gain visibility through red carpet experiences, media coverage, and distribution across She Rises Studios platforms, while connecting with a global network of women making an unstoppable impact.

NEXT FILMING OPPORTUNITIES

SHE WINS GLOBAL SUMMIT | LAS VEGAS | NOVEMBER 6–7, 2025
EMPOWERHER CONTENT DAY | LAS VEGAS | FEBRUARY 2026

SIGN UP TODAY

VISIT WWW.SHERISESSTUDIOS.COM/INTRODUCING-100-WOMEN-OF-IMPACT TO CLAIM YOUR SPOT.

THANK YOU TO OUR
EMPOWERHER
CONTENT DAY
GIFT BAG SPONSORS

We are deeply grateful to the 30+ brands who made EmpowerHER Content Day truly unforgettable. Your generosity, creativity, and support brought so much value to the experience.

Because of you, every attendee walked away inspired, connected, and empowered. Thank you for rising with us and being part of this impactful day.

THANK YOU TO OUR
EMPOWERHER
CONTENT DAY
SPONSORS

Keap

Put Your Marketing and Sales on Autopilot

https://keap.com/sherises

FENIX TV

From inspirational shows and expert interviews to empowering series and creative content.

https://fenixtv.app/

Sonya McDonald

Ignite Your Light, Transform Your Life

https://www.sonyamcdonald.com/

Sylvia Becker-Hill

Evolve through Neuro Creativity™
Feed Your Soul with Art

https://sylviabecker-hill.com/

Pure Heavenly

Extend Your Confidence
Lengthen Your Locks, Elevate Your Look

https://pureheavenlyhair.com/

Kline Hospitality

IGNITE TRANSFORMATION & PRODUCE GROWTH

https://www.klinehospitality.com/

Your support helps us empower women to rise and thrive.

THANK YOU TO OUR
EMPOWERHER
CONTENT DAY
GIFT BAG SPONSORS

Toothbrush Toys

Women-owned brand making brushing fun with reusable toothbrushes that double as collectible toys.

www.toothbrushtoys.com

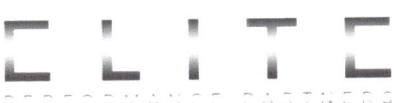

Elite Performance Partners, Inc.

Helping driven individuals achieve extraordinary results through science-backed coaching.

www.eliteperformancepartners.coach

She Wins Women's Network

Join a global movement of visionary women 50+ Chapters.

Growth.https://shewinswomensnetwork.com/

Brunch & Boss Up™

A live brunch show about real entrepreneurs, real stories, and boss-level energy

https://www.sherisesstudios.com/brunch-boss-up

She Rises Studios

A community where visibility, networking, and real connections help women create massive impac

thttps://www.sherisesstudios.com/introducing-100-women-of-impact

Lovful

A beauty brand creating hand-painted press-on nails that celebrate self-love, empowerment, and the strength of women.

https://www.lovful.com

Your support helps us empower women to rise and thrive.

THANK YOU TO OUR
EMPOWERHER CONTENT DAY
GIFT BAG SPONSORS

Soothi

A mindful stationery brand crafting handmade leather journals designed to inspire reflection, creativity, and purposeful living.

https://soothi.com

Lily Belle Boutique

Creates small-batch, non-toxic simmer pots made with real, visible ingredients for a safe and cozy home fragrance ritual.

www.lilybelleboutique.com

Skin Leaf Cosmetics

A clean beauty brand focused on minimalist skincare and sensorial elegance.

https://www.skinleaf.co

Suzy Levian New York

A jewelry and lifestyle brand built on legacy, resilience, and empowerment for women.

https://suzylevian.com

Get Uncomfortable or Change Course

Kelvin G. Abrams helps aspiring entrepreneurs face challenges with honesty, strategy, and mindset shifts.

https://www.kelvinabrams.com

Stellar Biotics LLC

A science-driven wellness brand creating all-natural immune and gut health supplements powered by del-IMMUNE V®.

https://stellarbiotics.com

Your support helps us empower women to rise and thrive.

THANK YOU TO OUR
EMPOWERHER
CONTENT DAY
GIFT BAG SPONSORS

HOTWORX

A global fitness franchise offering infrared sauna workouts that blend heat, energy, and exercise for a detoxifying training experience.

https://www.hotworx.net

The Functional Chocolate Company

Crafting delicious dark chocolate infused with functional ingredients to support everyday wellness.

https://funcho.co

Help A Reporter Out

HARO

Help A Reporter Out

https://www.helpareporter.com/

XO / Jacqui

XO Jacqui

Women-owned wellness brand making clean protein and supplements for women's changing bodies.

https://xojacqui.com

KISS & WEAR

Kiss & Wear

A playful, purpose-driven jewelry brand turning everyday style into a bold, joyful statement.

www.kissandwear.com

U
P
P
Y
!

Uppy!

Female-founded hydration brand helping travelers fight fatigue, jet lag, and dehydration with science-backed electrolytes.

uppylife.com

Your support helps us empower women to rise and thrive.

THANK YOU TO OUR
EMPOWERHER
CONTENT DAY
GIFT BAG SPONSORS

Harmony Haven

Sustainably made, modern kitchen towels that blend beauty, function, and everyday durability.

https://www.hhavenco.com

Rooted with Redd Coaching Services

Empowering individuals to embrace authenticity, prioritize mental wellness, and find strength through vulnerability.

www.achearedd.com

Sylver Consulting

We Empower brands, organizations and teams to lead transformation by bringing clarity and focus to the why, how and what of their future

https://sylverconsulting.com/

Bona Dea Naturals

A women-owned marketplace offering natural, hand-curated wellness products made by women, for women.

https://bonadeanaturals.com

All Things Elderberry

A women-owned wellness brand creating small-batch elderberry products to support immunity, energy, and everyday self-care.

www.allthingselderberry.com

Xpressive Mocha

Handmade skin and beard care crafted with coffee, tea, and plant-based ingredients to restore and nourish skin.

https://xpressivemocha.com

Your support helps us empower women to rise and thrive.

GRAB YOUR COPY NOW

Mindset Mastery: Unfunk Your Thinking, Rewire Your Brain, and Unlock Your Full Potential is a transformational guide for entrepreneurs, professionals, and leaders ready to break free from limitations and embrace bold new possibilities. Through powerful insights from thought leaders and high-performance experts, it reveals how to overcome mental blocks, rewire your thinking, and step into the mindset required for lasting success. Each chapter blends real stories, science-backed strategies, and actionable tools designed to build resilience, clarity, and confidence. With wisdom drawn from diverse experiences, this book reminds us that true growth begins when we shift our mindset and claim our full potential.

amazon.com   **SHE RISES**
S T U D I O S

COMMANDING POWER, UNLOCKING WEALTH, MASTERING EMPIRES:
THE *LISA STAMPER* EFFECT

In today's world, women are no longer waiting for permission to rise. They are stepping into their power, building empires, and rewriting the rules of success on their own terms. At the forefront of this movement is **Lisa Stamper**—a 7-figure entrepreneur, intuitive business strategist, high-ticket mentor, and best-selling author whose mission is to help ambitious women activate their highest potential and claim their place as leaders of the new economy.

Lisa's journey is more than an entrepreneurial success story —it's a blueprint for transformation. From humble beginnings, she carved out a global platform that now empowers women to build businesses aligned with both purpose and profit. She is the visionary founder of the **Evolve Community**, where women from around the world come together to expand wealth, confidence, and impact. She also created two groundbreaking frameworks—the **L.E.T. Method™** (Leadership, Embodiment, Transformation) and **The Millionaire Flow Protocol©**, both designed to help high-achievers break through plateaus, dissolve limiting beliefs, and master the art of scaling with soul.

Her work has not only been featured in Times Square but also in major media outlets, top podcasts, and global stages. She has inspired audiences at Harvard, UCLA, Oxford, and Cambridge, sharing the stage with luminaries like Jack Canfield and Deepak Chopra. What sets Lisa apart is her ability to combine **channeled wisdom** with **strategic business expertise**, making her both a guide and a catalyst for rapid results.

The Success Codes

Lisa is also the author of *The Success Codes*, a best-selling book that reveals the truth about real success while dismantling societal programming and deeply ingrained beliefs that hold people back. Ranked #5 on BookAuthority's *"20 Best New Success Books to Read in 2024,"* the book has been endorsed by transformational leaders like Marci Shimoff and continues to serve as a guide for women ready to claim more abundance, freedom, and authority in every area of their lives.

A New Era of Women's Wealth

Lisa Stamper represents a new wave of leadership in the Sheconomy—a world where women are not just participants but power players driving global markets, influence, and innovation.

She believes wealth is not simply financial—it's about embodiment, sovereignty, and the ability to create impact. Through her private mentorship and community programs, she teaches women how to command high-ticket sales with integrity, scale their businesses to six and seven figures, and lead with unshakable confidence.

For Lisa, it's not just about building empires; it's about creating **sustainable, soul-aligned success** that feels as good on the inside as it looks on the outside.

Why Lisa Matters Now

In 2025, as more women are entering entrepreneurship than ever before, the need for mentors who model both wealth and wellness is critical. Lisa's approach bridges the gap between intuitive mastery and practical strategy, giving women permission to do business differently—without burnout, hustle, or compromise. She empowers leaders to step out of survival and into their true evolution, activating creativity, courage, and conviction along the way.

Lisa Stamper is more than a mentor—she is a movement. A light for those ready to rise, she proves that when women own their power, they not only transform their own lives but also shift economies, industries, and legacies.

Connect With Lisa

www.LisaStamper.com
Instagram: @LisaStamperOfficial